LOLLIPOPS & LEMON SQUEEZERS

A NON-GROWN-UP'S RHYMING GUIDE TO LONDON

Mikey O'Crikey

Rhymes and doodles are copyright of Mikey O'Crikey. No part of this publication may be reproduced or transmitted in any form or by any means without the prior written permission of the author.

Any trademarks, service marks, product names or named features are assumed to be the property of their respective owners and are only used for reference. They are not endorsed by their use.

Copyright © 2021 Mikey O'Crikey
All rights reserved.

ISBN-13: 9798767817023

"In London, everyone is different and that means anyone can fit in."

– PADDINGTON BEAR

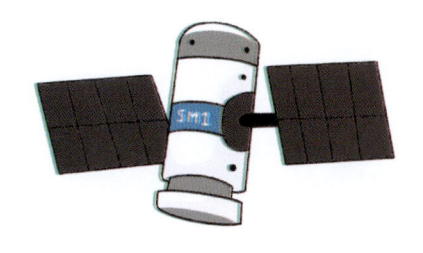

AUTHOR'S NOTE

I grew up in what was once a 'satellite town' of London. Sadly that doesn't mean satellites were made there (that would have been nifty!). Rather it means it was a town close to the city but not part of it. As the capital expanded, and long before I came along, my hometown became a London suburb.

I now live closer to the city centre. And, though I moved here and there in between, London has always been my home. A place, as Paddington Bear rightly observed, where everyone is different and anyone can fit in. A town that's often exciting and sometimes frustrating but never boring. A right old well of inspiration!

And so here we are with this collection - my take on some of the things about the city that I find brilliant or bonkers. That said, I do hope it can be enjoyed by non-grown-ups (of all ages) wherever in the world you are from or find yourself.

And maybe it'll provoke you ponder on the brilliant and bonkers things about a place you know. In fact, there's a space at the end of the book for you to write a rhyme or draw a doodle about it - or both! Go on, have a go...

RHYME-DOODLE MAP

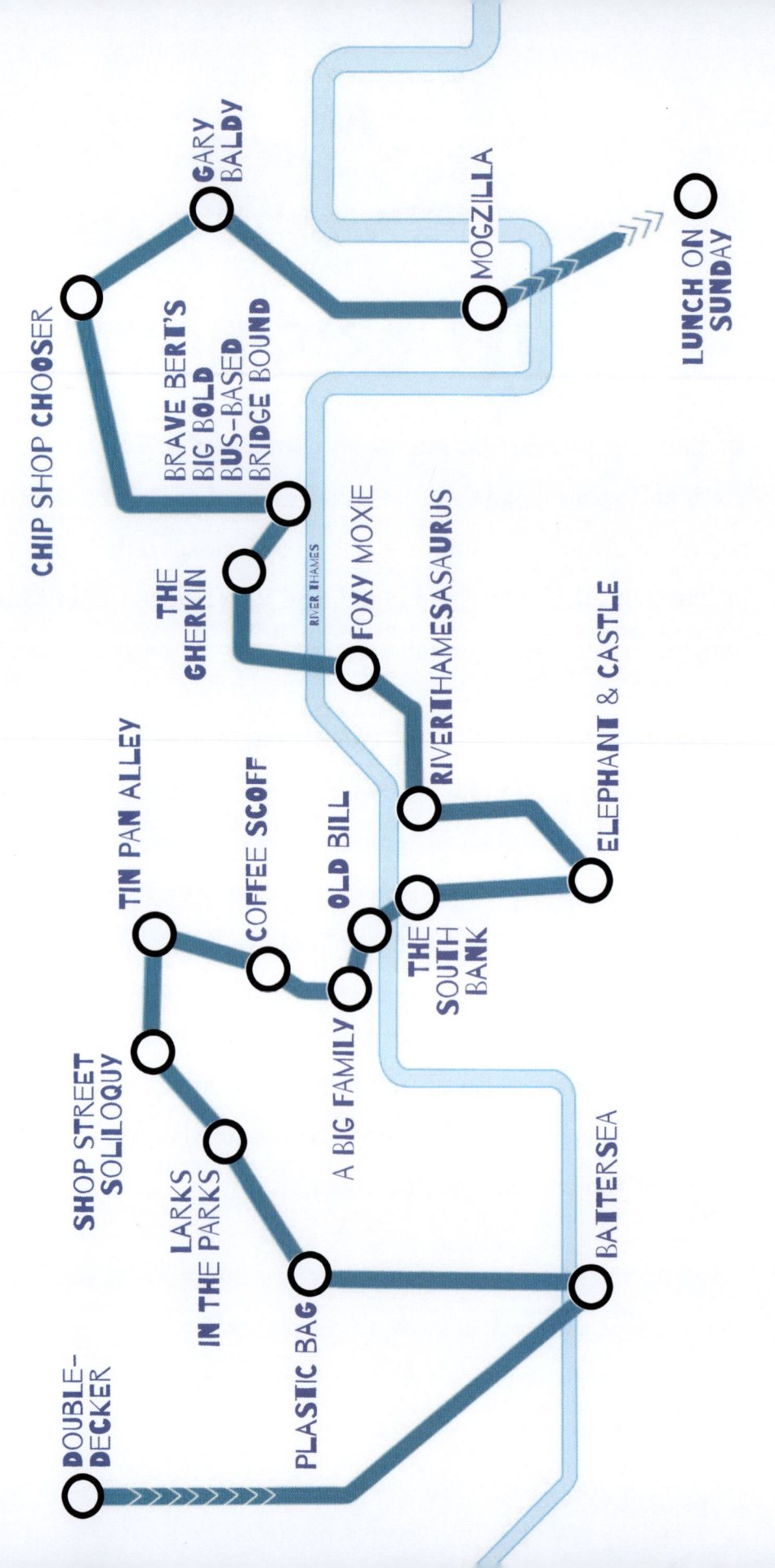

- GARY BALDY
- CHIP SHOP CHOOSER
- BRAVE BERT'S BIG BOLD BUS-BASED BRIDGE BOUND
- THE GHERKIN
- MOGZILLA
- LUNCH ON SUNDAY
- FOXY MOXIE
- RIVER THAMES
- RIVERTHAMESASAURUS
- ELEPHANT & CASTLE
- TIN PAN ALLEY
- COFFEE SCOFF
- OLD BILL
- THE SOUTH BANK
- SHOP STREET SOLILOQUY
- LARKS IN THE PARKS
- A BIG FAMILY
- PLASTIC BAG
- BATTERSEA
- DOUBLE-DECKER

- DOUBLE-DECKER — 1
- BATTERSEA — 3
- PLASTIC BAG — 5
- LARKS IN THE PARKS — 7
- SHOP STREET SOLILOQUY — 9
- TIN PAN ALLEY — 11
- COFFEE SCOFF — 13
- A BIG FAMILY — 15
- OLD BILL — 17
- THE SOUTH BANK — 19
- ELEPHANT & CASTLE — 21
- RIVERTHAMESASAURUS — 23
- FOXY MOXIE — 25
- THE GHERKIN — 27
- BRAVE BERT'S BIG BOLD BUS-BASED BRIDGE BOUND — 29
- CHOP SHOP CHOOSER — 31
- GARY BALDY — 33
- MOGZILLA — 35
- LUNCH ON SUNDAY — 37

DOUBLE-DECKER

Squeeze down the tube or hire a bike,
Hail a black taxi if you like.
But to cross town, well *I* do so thus:
On a big red double-decker bus.

Weighing in about a dozen ton,
You can hold them up with just your thumb,
As the driver sees your sky-raised finger,
On the kerb-side you need no longer linger.

On boarding I always head upstairs,
(The low deck's for old folks and pushchairs),
Where hopefully I bag a window seat,
The best tour you'll get of London's streets.

The only way it could be better
Was if they rose to triple-decker.
One more floor in which to squidge,
P'raps a problem though when bus meets bridge?

Looking for a variety of views?
Well, there's hundreds of routes from which to choose.
Just avoid sure traveller dejection
By boarding in the right direction.

To Piccadilly from High Street Ken?
Flag down the number 9 (not 10).
And Hampstead down to Pimlico?
The 24's the way to go.

My favourite course to Britain's Tate
Is on the top deck of the 88.
Of course, its numerically bisected route
Will take you down from Vic to Toot.

Any place in town that you could name,
From Bread Street through to Pudding Lane,
To find a way you won't be troubled,
Catch a big red bus whose decks are doubled.

Not many things shout 'London!' like a red double-decker bus. And, on the top deck of one is hands down the best way to cross town. Don't be put off by traffic jams - all the more time to stare out of the window at whatever odd things are happening down in the streets below.

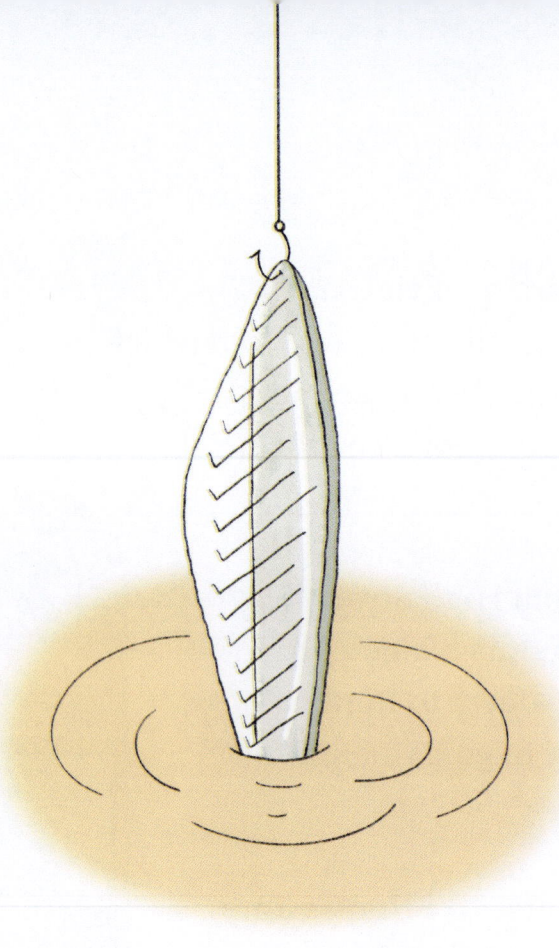

BATTERSEA

In Battersea, Battersea, go dip your cod,
Then into hot oil with a sizzle-proof rod.
Serve with thick chips and a sprinkle of salt,
Dowse it in lemon or vinegar (malt).

Of Battersea, Battersea, craft Yorkshire puddies,
Roast them with spuds and other root goodies.
And into the core of this savoury treat,
Pour some hot gravy - très bon appétit!

With Battersea, Battersea be sure to make,
A perfectly circular, griddled pancake.
Flip it and flap it and flop it back down,
Don't toss it too high lest it land on your crown.

But Battersea, Battersea, from you must keep clear,
All of your digits, your tongue, nose and ear.
As in one thing for certain we all are allied,
Appendages are better off not southern fried.

This book is partly inspired by 'Nursery Rhymes of London Town' by Eleanor Farjeon. Eleanor's collection takes a wry look at place names in the city - including a rhyme about Battersea. Published over 100 years ago, it is still a fun read today.

PLASTIC BAG

Plastic bag stuck in a tree,
How come that's where you came to be?
Were you hurled there by a dumbo?
Or plummet from a passing jumbo?

Did you catch a rising thermal gust?
Or whipped up there by a speeding bus?
Were you a parachute for an Action Man?
Are you polythene's answer to Tarzan?

Plastic bag stuck in a tree,
What can you see that we can't see?
Bald patches of the lankiest men?
Who pass beneath you now and then?

Can you see down into prams,
Top decks of buses, roofs of trams?
Or upwards to the underneath
Of pigeons' nethers? Oh, good grief!

Plastic bag stuck in a tree,
What on earth will become of thee?
Disintegrate as you get all drab
And fall in some poor bloke's kebab?

Will you break free and fly on high,
Right up into the big blue sky?
Find a window and drift right in,
End up in someone's kitchen bin?

Plastic rubbish is bad. We all know that. And plastic bags are among the worst kind. But this rhyme came about when I saw a tree with plastic bags as leaves at an art exhibition. It got me thinking about those plastic bags you often see stuck in trees - especially in cities like London - and what their view on city life might be...

LARKS IN THE PARKS

Oh I do love to wander the parks,
I have the most extraordinary larks.
But though many have ponds,
Through the weeds and the fronds,
I have yet to detect any sharks.

I like one with a farm or a zoo,
And in London there's more than a few.
Though it's easy to make,
A uncleanly mistake,
As you tiptoe round all of the poo.

If there's a heatwave you want to expunge,
There are lakes into which you can plunge.
May get mud between toes,
Or pond slime up your nose,
So try a lido if you'd rather no gunge.

Near a tree I am wont to recline,
Bring a picnic on which one can dine.
But make sure the frittata
And that posh chipolata,
Aren't scoffed by a passing canine.

Oh to have parks in the midst of a city,
Makes them even more special and pretty.
Though the civil by-laws,
Means that all dinosaurs,
Must be models not real, more's the pity.

You see I tell you there's no greater place,
To take life at a leisurely pace,
Or have rollicking fun,
In the snow or in sun,
Than in a London fair city green space.

Cities are sometimes described as 'concrete jungles'. But in London we are lucky to have so many large green spaces - from commons to royal parks, wetlands to great gardens, heaths to recreation grounds. Few better places to kick a ball around, have a picnic or just simply go for a stroll.

SHOP STREET SOLILOQUY

I used to be a Roman road,
A highway of cobblestone.
But now two-millenia later
I'm a tarmaced shopping zone.

You can buy all sorts on me,
A nice dress a funny hat,
Bones and biscuits for your dog,
A jewelled tiara for your cat.

At one end of me's a tower,
At the other there's an arch.
And at nearly two kilometres
I can be quite the tiring march.

Cabs and buses can drive down me,
Or if you're a bike, okay.
But try to cruise down on a jet ski,
Never, not allowed, no way!

At my middle there's a circus,
Roll up and take a pew!
Now, have you seen the ringmaster?
And that tightrope walker too?

I cross paths with a regent
And a spy with double Os.
I'm notorious for pollution,
Hold your breath and pinch your nose.

I'm so famous that at Christmas
I'm literally up in dazzling lights.
So even astronauts can pinpoint me
On those dark and wintry nights.

But I'm probably most well-known
As a street chock-full of shops,
Outlets, stores, emporia
Or, in cockney, 'lollipops'.

A soliloquy is when you speak your mind but it doesn't matter if anyone's there to hear it. This street is a very busy one so doesn't have to worry about that - plenty of people round to hear! But do you know its name..?

(PS - can you spot the cat in a jewelled tiara somewhere in this book..?)

TIN PAN ALLEY

My dad's brought me up to London
To the famous Tin Pan Alley.
We're here to pick an instrument,
Right, let's not dilly-dally!

Will I be a pianist
And play piano like a pro?
Perhaps the xylophone or glockenspiel?
I don't plinky-plonk think so.

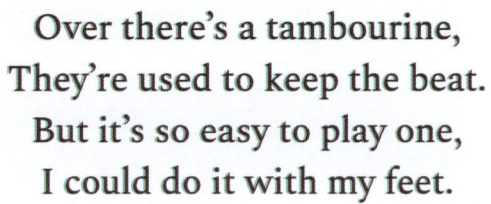

Over there's a tambourine,
They're used to keep the beat.
But it's so easy to play one,
I could do it with my feet.

Perhaps I'll be a drummer,
I like to thump and bash.
I'd really love a bass guitar,
But we just haven't got the cash.

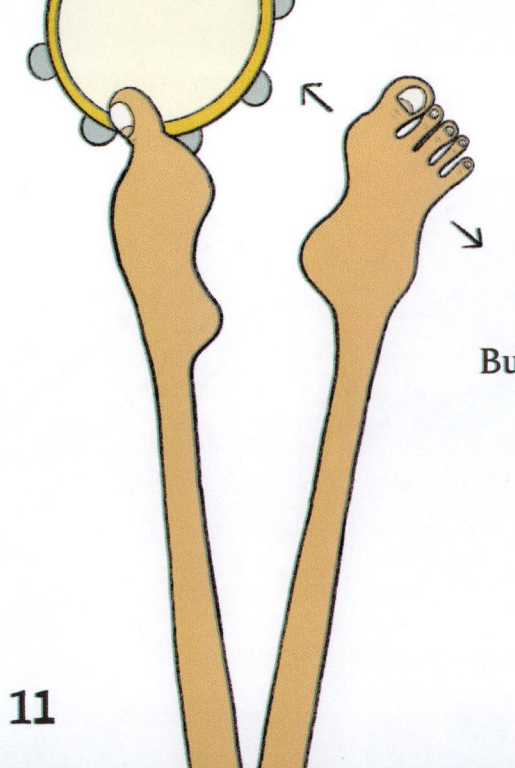

Maybe then the triangle,
For they are not that dear at all.
Though Rod already plays that
In the orchestra at school.

How about the violin,
Accordion or harp?
Or I could play the trumpet,
I mean, who doesn't like a parp?

I might learn the clarinet,
Oboe or saxophone.
I could play it extra loud
To make my big sis groan.

Oh no, not a recorder!
My dad says it's a classic.
What he learnt at school, he says.
Well, how utterly jurassic!

I used to visit Tin Pan Alley (official name - Denmark Street) occasionally with my bros growing up. Mostly to check out all the guitars that were well out of our pocket money range. I eventually bought an instrument from a Tin Pan Alley shop - a ukulele. Bit trendier than a recorder.

COFFEE SCOFF

There are these shops all over town,
They'll make you scoff, they'll make you frown,
For though they put great care in coffee,
They cannot make good tea for toffee.

First of all let's take the blends,
Some so bland they will offend
Both dabbler and the connoisseur;
Far from teapot cordon bleu.

Next consider the size of cup;
So huge that just to pick it up,
Almost requires super powers,
And will keep you in the loo for hours.

But worst of all, their analysis
Of 'a dash of milk' is quite remiss;
They pour enough to drain an udder.
Milky tea? Don't make me shudder!

No naming names. You know who they are, I know who they are, they know who they are. A tad more care with our national drink, please!

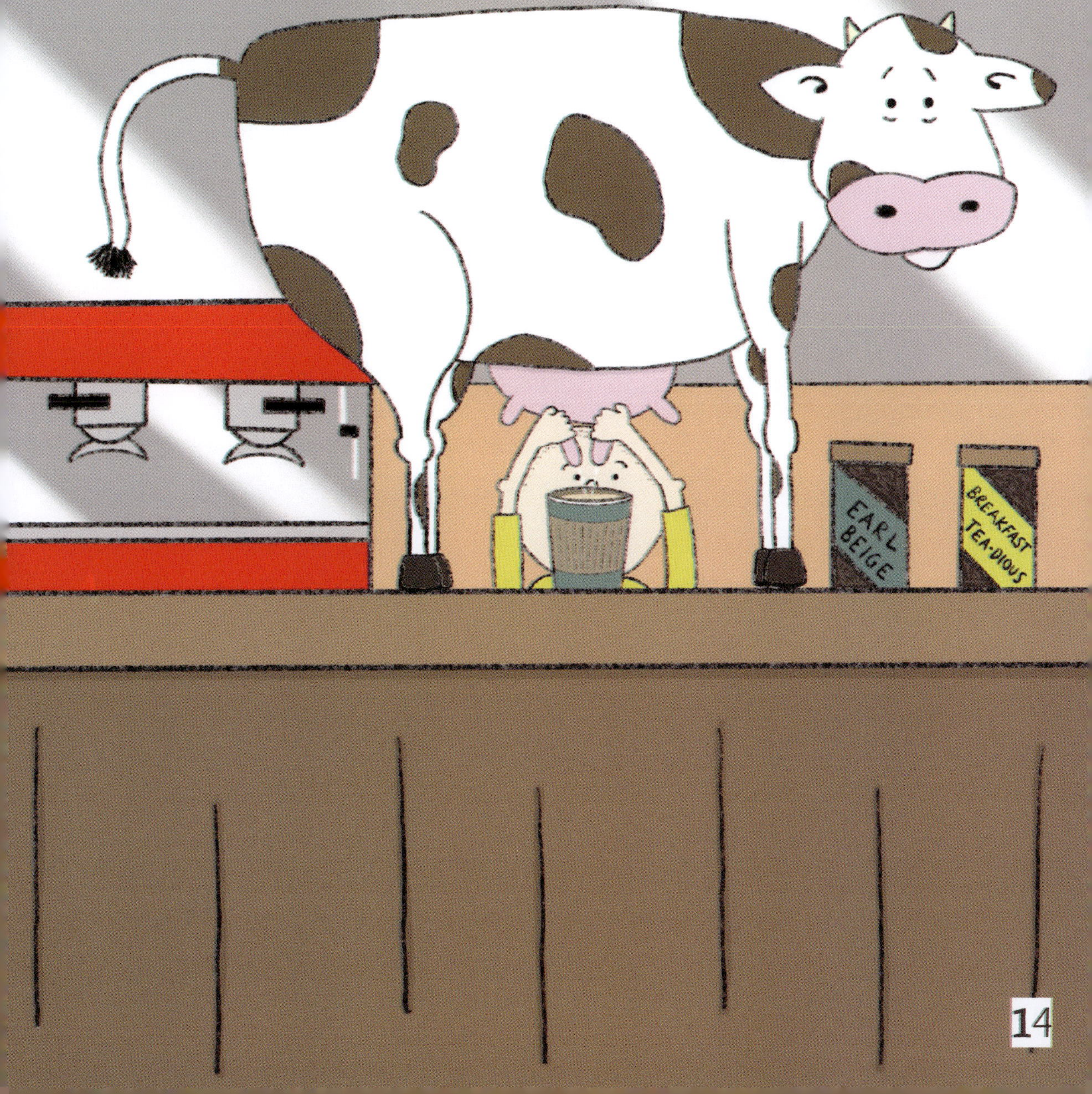
EARL BEIGE
BREAKFAST TEA-DIOUS

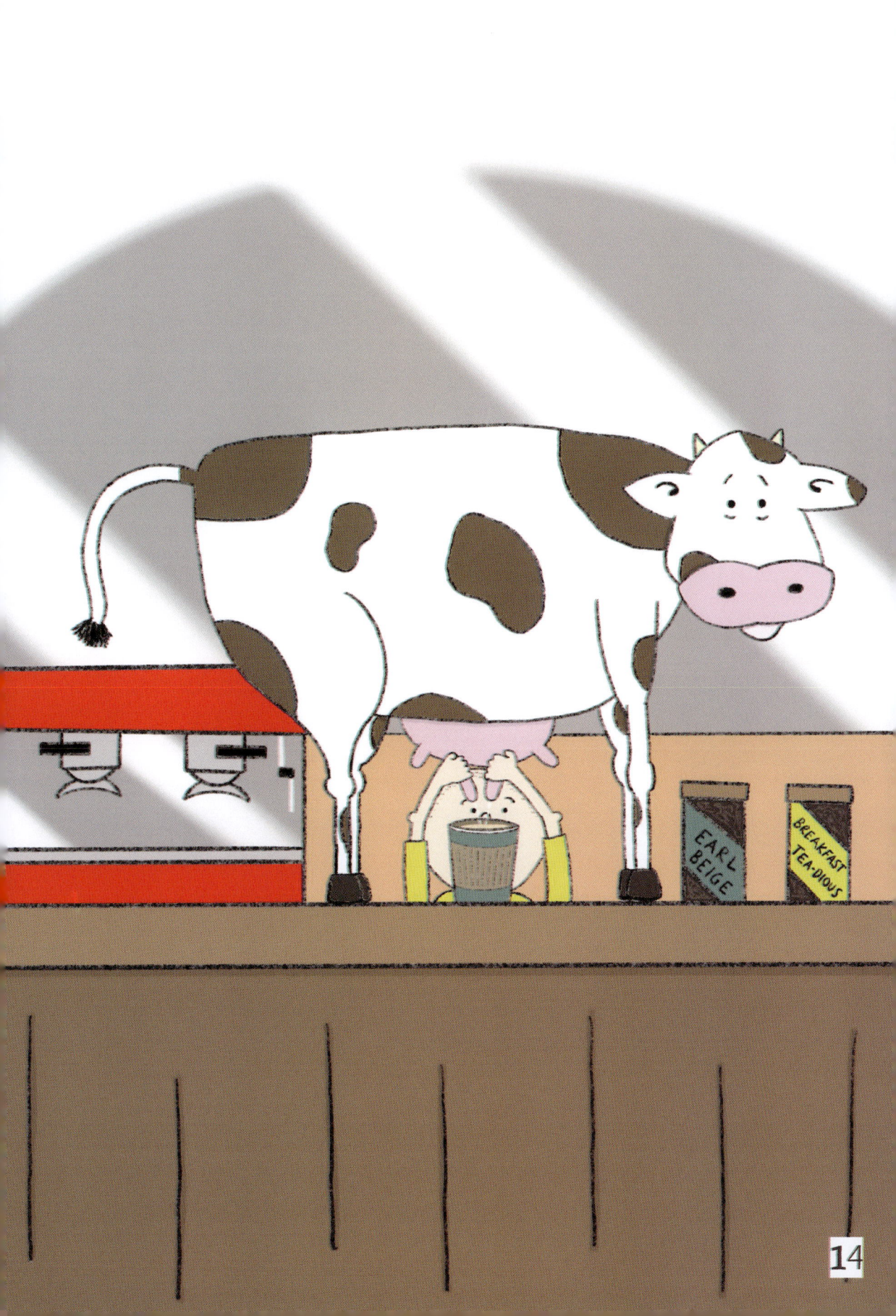

A BIG

Big Ben, Big Ben...

Little Bro to Larger Jen...

Who's sister is Humungous Gwen...

Both cousins of Galactic Sven...

FAMILY

Lad and lass of Massive Ken...　　And grandkids of Enormous Len...

A clan who find it tricky when...　　...finding space for a reunion.

Strictly speaking, London's Big Ben is the largest bell in the clock tower rather than the tower itself (as every bore will tell you). But it's the tower that you think of when you hear that name, right? Of course it is, mate.

OLD BILL

Old Bill the bobby buffs his boots for the beat,
Assuring their shine survives his shift on the streets.
Tightens his tie and tucks tummy in trews,
Bedecked from his bonce to his boxers in blue.

He plods and parades and patrols round his patch,
Combing for crims, crooks and conmen to catch.
He grabs and he grapples with gangsters and geezers,
Or, in local lingo, lawless 'lemon squeezers'.

Safely and skillfully between sidewalks he steers
Dawdlers and dodderers and indebted old dears.
To galleries he guides got-lost globetrotters galore,
Shows shoppers to shops and shoplifters the score.

A day's duty delivered, with deserved delectation
He scoffs swiftly his supper served a-steam at the station.
Then tipples with tea, his toppermost treat,
Old boy in blue Bill, bobby on the beat.

The original headquarters of the Metropolitan Police was called 'Scotland Yard'. It moved in 1890 and was renamed 'New Scotland Yard'. It moved again in 1967 and became 'New New Scotland Yard'. Then in 2016 it moved again to become 'New New New Scotland Yard'. But that's too many 'New's so they decided to lose two 'New's and now choose to use only one 'New'. Phew!

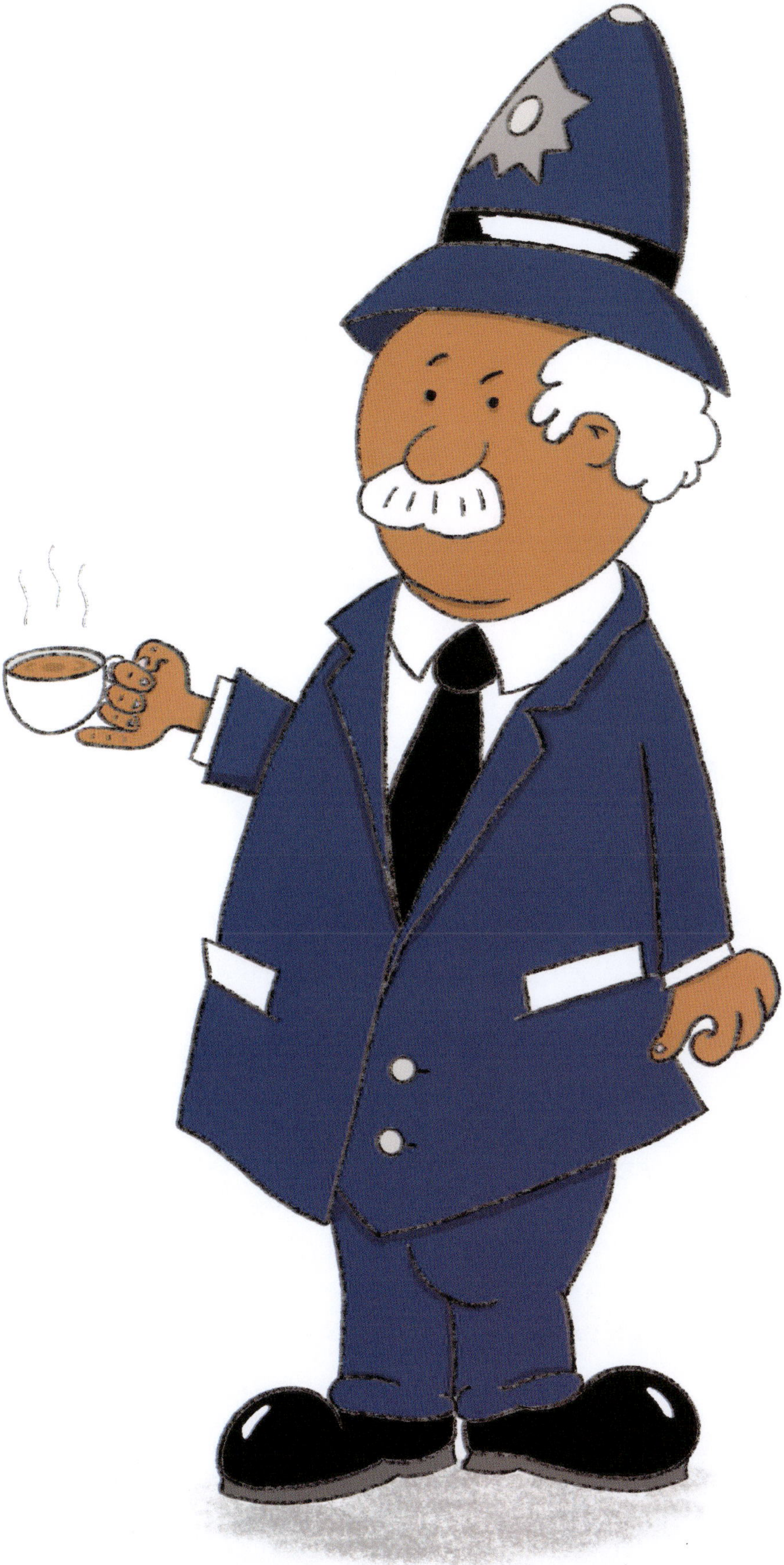

THE SOUTH BANK

I went down to the South Bank
To make a cash deposit;
I'd decided it was high time that
I moved it from my closet.

Alas, when I arrived there,
No depository to find.
But restaurants, shops, a giant wheel
And sights of other kinds.

I found cinemas and theatres,
One that looked four centuries old.
And a little nook where people stood
On small wheeled planks and rolled.

A great big hulking edifice,
Named for a sugar king.
Where those handy with a paintbrush
Display arty-crafty things.

Leafleters and buskers,
Rows of books beneath a bridge,
Food stalls to feed me for a week,
Though I'll need a deeper fridge!

So lots of ways to spend my cash
But no place in which to hoard it.
I'll just have to find another bank
Or maybe buy a bigger closet.

There's good reason why this stretch of riverside is always busy. Its mix of art, culture, food and entertainment brings all of London's greatness together in one narrow mile or so. With none of the boring stuff. Like banks.

ELEPHANT & CASTLE

Your local zoo, the safari park,
Dawdling by two off of Noah's ark.
In the African or Indian wild, yeah sure,
But no pachyderms are living in the house next door.

No trumpet calls, no prehensile conks,
No droppings more massive that you've seen in yonks.
The biggest ears I've seen were on that couple at the deli,
But he didn't look a dumbo and she sure was no nelly.

A palace here, a mansion there,
Many seats of power for your derrière.
Lots of grand old houses in the town, it's true,
But there's no ancient fortress in these parts to view.

No stagnant moat, no lookout posts,
No dark dungeons cast with horrid rats and ghosts.
Never round here you'll see a drawbridge fall,
So why did they name it as they did at all?!

> The answer to the question at the end of this rhyme is, it was named after a pub. But how the pub got its name, no one knows. Not really anyway - though there are theories. Pub names are mysterious things! What's clear is it's a bonkers name for a place. And you have to love it for that.

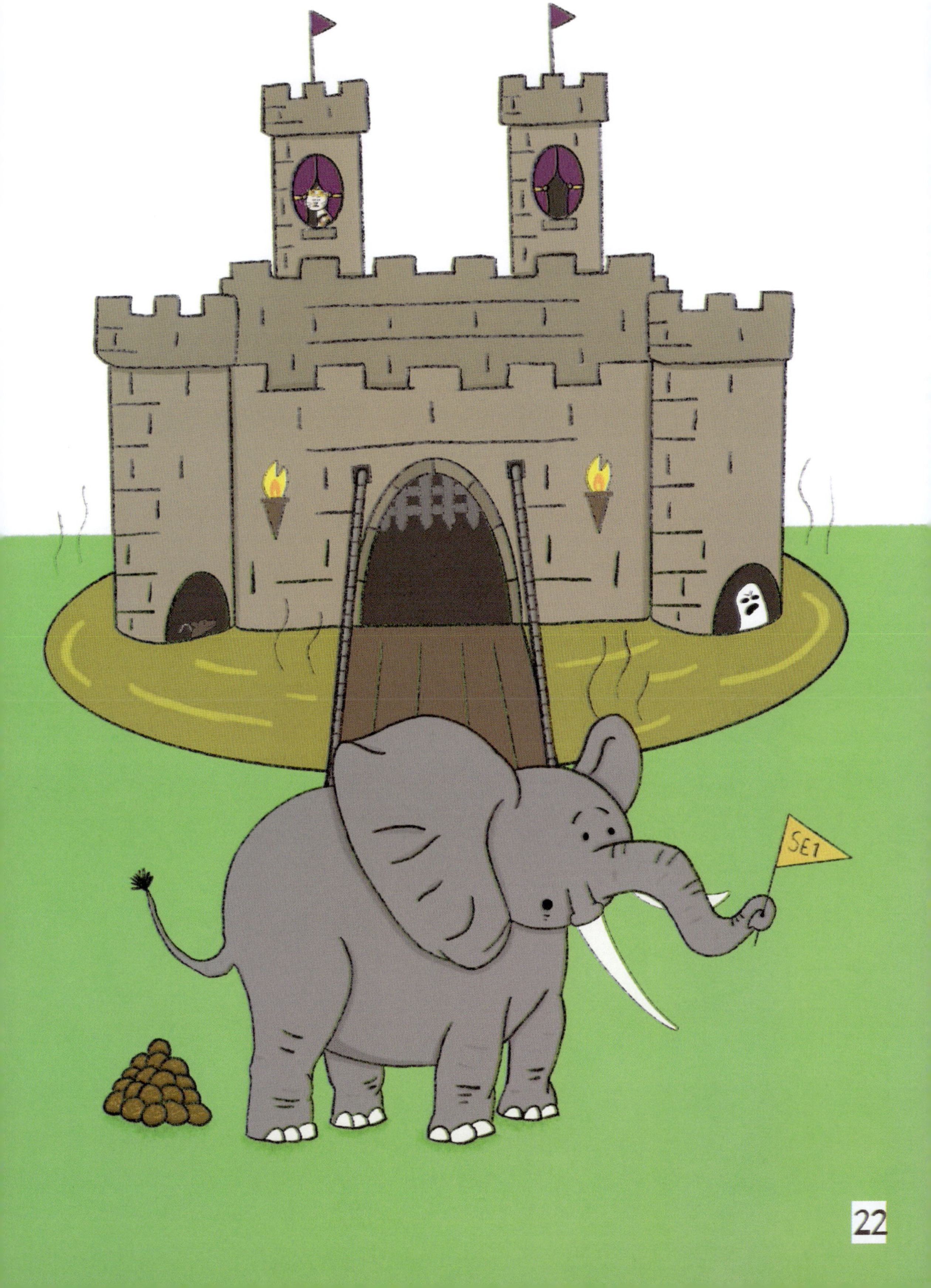
SE1

RIVERTHAMESASAURUS

We were walking along the riverside,
A beach had appeared, it was low tide.
Without delay and on a whim,
We jumped down for a pebble skim.

No sooner were we on the shore,
You will not believe what we then saw.
Scattered among the sand and stones,
Three-toed tracks and small dark bones.

The only time we'd clocked bones this shade,
And such footsteps in the shoreline made,
Is when we'd been on museum tours
Of exhibitions on dinosaurs.

"What a stroke of luck", I said,
"Dinos! Seems both alive and dead!"
My chum and I exclaimed in chorus,
"We'll name it Riverthamesasaurus!"

We snapped the tracks and bagged the bones,
Abandoned our game of skimming stones,
Jumped on a bus, where we did proclaim,
"Take us to fortune and fame!"

Luckily we'd picked a westward route,
And no sooner, with our prehistoric loot,
We were in the Natural History Museum,
The world's top dino mausoleum.

We found an expert in a peaked blue hat,
"Bird tracks," he said, "bones of a rat."
I twigged then he was a security guard,
Too late - he slung us out to the yard.

We retraced our steps and dumped the bones,
Went back to our game of skimming stones,
When I saw a glinting in the sun,
"Look, treasure from a Spanish galleon..!"

This actually happened. Well, part of it did - when I was down at the Thames river line with my buddy Patrick one day. Wandering along, we spotted them - three-toed tracks and small dark bones. We were convinced they were from a dino. Well, I was anyway. I think Patrick was less sure.

FOXY MOXIE

Romeo, Romeo, wherefore art thou?
Climbed that skyscraper? Oh blimey! Oh wow!
Well, I guess up at floor number 72
You are guaranteed an extraordinary view.

This isn't that chap from old Will's tragic play;
He's not from these parts (and made up anyway).
This is the true tale of a very brave foxy,
Who really did have some magnificent moxie.

You see as The Shard was still being upraised,
This venturesome vulpine, completely unfazed,
Skulked in through a gap, claiming new territory,
Right up there aloft on that sky-high storey.

Now they say that foxes are cunning and sly,
So did he head for the stairs or give it a try
To make his ascent less tiring, more swift,
By pressing the button to call down the lift?

If he did do the latter, we never will know
(Though I do like to think he at least had a go).
Whatever his route up, there's really no doubt,
He was clearly the loftiest canine about.

For what reason to climb high over the town...
To spy on the streets 800 feet down?
Was he up looking for his Juliet?
Could it be the result of a dare or a bet?

Well, possibly just like you or like me,
What he actually went all that way up to see,
Was that urban perspective (it's truly a winner),
Or just how much the restaurant will charge you for dinner.

Whatever his reason, he eventually was found,
Then taken right back all the way to the ground.
For Romeo, a return to a life on the street,
And but only to dream of his tall foxy feat!

There is something wonderful, almost magical, about having foxes living in our urban areas. London has some of the bravest and most streetwise of the species. And none more so than this real life Romeo and his cunning climb above the capital.

THE GHERKIN

Look at that great big gherkin!
I love a gherkin, me.
I especially like a slice inside
A burger for my tea.

Are there other city sights
Named after pickled food?
Or was the architect of this
In a slightly funny mood?

Is there a big beetroot bridge
Or a castle cornichon?
Not seen super silverskins
On my walks out in London.

What about XL pickled eggs,
Even bigger than a chip shop?
That would be the sort of thing
To make a chutney-chewing jaw drop!

Right, that's it, I have a plan now,
It'll be my lifelong purpose
To log all these spots - I'll make a start
With Piccalilli Circus.

London has a special knack for giving its biggest buildings nicknames. I love that one of them is named after a pickled vegetable, of all things. One of my favourite pickled vegetables. Defo top three.

BRAVE BERT'S BIG BOLD

Across town many a year ago,
In '52 to be exact,
Albert Gunter set off for work,
With his lucky lunchbox packed.

What he did not know then
Was he'd soon become a ledge,
For running eight thousand kilos
Off a slowly rising edge.

To fill a gap in the story,
If you've not already understood,
Brave Bert was a bus-driver
Round London's east end neighbourhoods.

On that fateful day he helmed
The number 78.
His uttermost concern of course
Was to make no punters late.

BUS-BASED BRIDGE BOUND

Now, as he crossed old Tower Bridge
On his way up to Shoreditch,
The road that ran beneath him
Set upon a worrying pitch.

You see the hapless bloke whose job it was
To ring the bell and shut the gate,
Was lazy or distracted,
Or back from his loo break late.

A split-second choice Bert had to make
And he slammed his right foot down,
To reach the heady 12 miles per hour,
Make the greatest leap in town.

Well, he landed with all passengers safe
And not a scratch on that routemaster!
So, the reward for this true hero?
Ten quid, a day off, his leg in plaster.

Bridges are great structures and the Thames has lots of them of course. Tower Bridge is a particularly marvellous example - and this true story of Bert's bus-based bound seals its spot among the most marvellous bridges in the world.

CHIP SHOP CHOOSER

Haddock or coley or pollock or plaice,
Mackerel or kippers to stuff in your face.
We've all sorts of fish caught with net or with rod!
No thank you sir, I'm happy with cod.

Cockles or mussels or winkles or squid,
Crayfish or lobster, if you have a few quid.
All sorts of creatures scooped out of the sea!
No thanks very much, it's a large cod for me.

Sausage or saveloy, pasty or pie,
Burger or nuggets, if you're that kind of guy.
We've even got goujons for the la-di-da kind!
I'm having the cod mate, I've made up my mind!

Falafel with hummus, a hot mushroom slice,
Corn on the cob or in fritter (quite nice).
For veggies and vegans we cater, don't worry!
You know what, I actually fancy a curry...

So, though other parts of the country may dispute it, there is good evidence that the first official fish and chip shop was opened in Bow, east London in 1860. Joseph Malin, a seller of fried fish, had the bright idea to combine this traditional Jewish-Portuguese delight with the classic native fare of chipped potatoes. And so, in the magnificent melting pot that is our capital city, our beloved national dish was born!

Cod	Cockles	Sausage	Falafel ....
Haddock	Mussels	Saveloy	Hummus ....
Coley	Winkles	Pasty	Hot mushroom
Pollock	Squid	Pie	slice ....
Plaice	Crayfish	Burger	Corn on cob ...
Mackerel	Lobster	Nuggets	Corn fritter ....
Kippers		Goujons	

CODSWALLOP

GARY BALDY

They called him Gary Baldy,
He was as hairless as an egg.
Shoplifted squashed fly biscuits,
Hid them down his trouser legs.

He hung around with petty crims
Who hobnobbed in the pubs.
Played poker for their booty.
Gary's lucky suit - the clubs.

Well, the coppers, they did cop him
And they took him down the nick.
Interviewed by DI Gestive,
Who couldn't get the charge to stick.

For he was a right old jammy dodger,
With his endless crooked schemes.
Once he'd pinched all the squashed fly biscuits
He just moved on to custard creams.

Londoners love a nickname. They also like a biscuit. Some of them can be proper dodgy 'lemon squeezers'. This rhyme is all those things squashed together - a bit like the squashed fly biscuit it's named after.

DISCLAIMER: Mikey O'Crikey neither condones nor wishes to make light of shoplifting. On the contrary, it's a very bad idea all round. Not least because you're bound to put you back out trying to lift a shop.

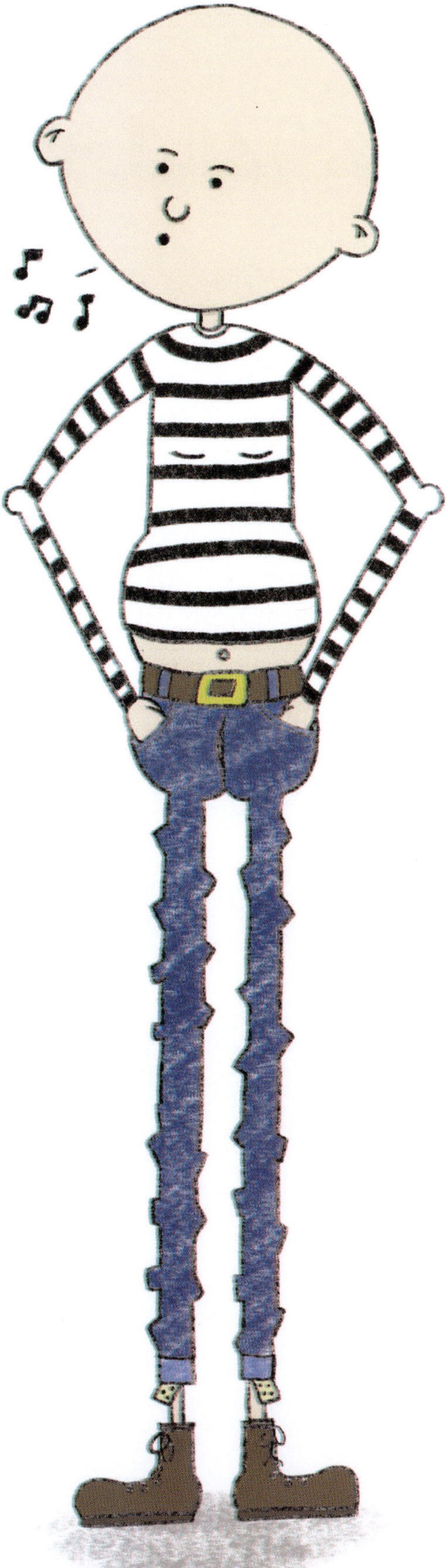

MOGZILLA

A terror has overthrown the deep,
So best silence your budgie's every peep.
As even a hundred foot gorilla
Won't deter the towering Mogzilla!

She's stomped her way right up the river,
Sent pets and people alike ashiver.
Her aim, this behemoth of mogs:
To obliterate the Isle of Dogs.

A few brave pooches, mutts and hounds
Have gathered there to stand their ground.
Their barks and snarls engulf the city,
As they fight back against this monster kitty.

Can they drive back their feline foe?
Or their island will she overthrow?
We'll know one day, there is no doubt,
When, inevitably, the movie's out...

Two funny things about the Isle of Dogs: 1) it may not actually be named after dogs at all - one of the theories about its name is that it's meant to be 'Isle of Ducks' from when it was a marshland; and 2) it's not even an island - it's actually a peninsula! Not that either point would deter the Queen of the Mogsters from her invasion, of course!

36

LUNCH ON SUNDAY

"Ooo a' yoo?" she would always say
When we went round on a Sunday,
Standing guard at the front door,
Pretending she'd not seen us before.

They grew up the old cockney way,
My nan and grandad, I should say.
So the odd consonant they'd drop
And occasionally use a glottal stop.

Well, we would laugh and smile and grin,
And eventually Nan would let us in,
Where Grandad would be cooking lunch
For us inevitably hungry bunch.

They'd pile the meat and 'taters high,
"Ere 'av another, don't be shy!"
But the best thing, giant Yorkshire puds,
Enough gravy to flood neighbourhoods.

Up in London, Grandad sold flowers
But really he had super powers.
Could chew roast pork and cracklin'
Without his set of dentures in.

A funny face then Nan would pull
And we'd try to keep in our mouthful,
As at her silliness we'd snigger,
Our grins growing bigger and bigger.

Both born within the Bow Bells peals,
Bet they'd scoffed tons of jellied eels.
But we, their more fastidious kin,
We're happy they'd not serve those for dins.

Yes, glad instead with a roast beef,
In which we'd happily sink our teeth.
Then with bellies bulging beneath our shirts,
Lime jelly and ice cream for our desserts.

My nan and grandad's names were Kit and Bert and they were both very funny. They were true cockneys, having been born and grown up in that particular part of the east end of London. Though by the time my siblings and I were knocking about, they'd long been living in the suburbs, in the house that our dad and aunts grew up in. This is the house in the rhyme and these are some of the events, as I remember them, of our Sunday visits.

BEFORE I GO...

So, there you go. My personal take on the brilliant and bonkers things that make London the special place it is. Maybe you learnt a new thing or two and hopefully you sniggered once or twice...

But most of all I hope it has made you think about a place you know and love in a bit of a different way. Enough to inspire you to write your own silly rhyme or draw your own daft doodle..?

I've left you a few pages at the end of book here to do just that. But before you start, a few tips: arm yourself with a reliable thesaurus and a stout pencil, don't over think your ideas and remember to have fun.

And I'd love to see the rhymes and doodles that you come up with. So please do send me copies, scans or pics of your work if you're up for sharing. Get in touch with me at:

mikeyocrikey.com

instagram.com/mikeyocrikey

twitter.com/mikeyocrikey

facebook.com/mikeyocrikey

ABOUT THE AUTHOR

Mikey O'Crikey, grew up in the outskirts of south London, with his mum and dad and three siblings. They lived happily in their small house, which had a big garden where Mikey and his brothers and sister loved to play.

Mikey has lived in west London, south-west London and even smack bang in the middle of central London, near to the West End. He now lives on the southern edge of central London (near to a place in one of this book's rhymes), with his partner, Clare and their best cat pal, Wilma.

ALSO BY THE AUTHOR...

Recycled Parsnips

Rhymes and doodles for non-grown-ups

Collective Memories

Wild rhymes and doodles for non-grown-ups

Printed in Great Britain
by Amazon